SUPERSPIC

ALBERT ORTIZ

SUPERSPIC

iUniverse books may be ordered through booksellers or by contacting:

iUniverse
1663 Liberty Drive
Bloomington, IN 47403
www.iuniverse.com
844-349-9409

ISBN: 978-1-6632-4928-9 (sc)
ISBN: 978-1-6632-4929-6 (e)

Library of Congress Control Number: 2022923658

Print information available on the last page.

iUniverse rev. date: 12/22/2022

CHAPTER 1

The Bronx is a place that has seen its share of famous singers, and actors. Stories like a Bronx Tale and singing groups like Dion and the Belmonts, Larry Chance and the Earls. Then there is me. Though not famous, I am the successful product of a single mom, raising three children with very little money. We all made it, thanks to her. The title of my book will probably get some people offended or insulted, especially today, with the diplomatically correct nonsense going on, but it is being used to describe me and no one else. I don't use it to offend, but to motivate and inspire others.

In 1973, my senior year at DeWitt Clinton High School, I was picked to play the lead role in a school play. The play was put on by a Puerto Rican youth social group. It was the story of someone coming from the hills (Jibaro) of Puerto Rico, arriving in New York City and being in awe of the big city. He then gets attack by a couple of individuals, and when they tear off his shirt they find a superspic shirt underneath. I continued using the name Superspic and when someone did or does call me a spic, I corrected them by saying "No, I am superspic". This deflates the bigot who thought he was going to use it to insult me. I have used SuperSpic several times in my life. I will continue to use it

1

AND I DON'T CARE IF IT'S NOT POLITICALLY CORRECT. JOIN ME ON MY JOURNEY OR DON'T. I HOPE YOU DO.

I WAS BORN IN NEW YORK CITY, AT THE OLD HARLEM HOSPITAL ON THE 4TH OF JULY 1955. I AM PROUD TO SAY THAT I AM A NEW YORK RICAN. MY MOTHER WAS GENOVEVA MORALES-ALEJANDRO, BORN ON THE 20TH OF JANUARY, 1929, IN RIO ALTO, LAS PIEDRAS, PUERTO RICO. I HAVE TWO YOUNGER SISTERS NAMED SONIA AND NANCY. I WILL BE USING THE TERM "MAMI" IN THIS STORY BECAUSE THAT IS WHAT WE ALWAYS CALLED OUR MOM. THE INFORMATION I WRITE ABOUT MAMI, WAS THE INFORMATION MAMI GAVE ME BECAUSE I ALWAYS MADE SURE I ASKED AND WROTE DOWN INFORMATION ABOUT HER.

SHE WAS MY MOM AND DAD AND I ALWAYS THANKED HER FOR BEING WHO SHE WAS AND RAISING ME TO BE A MAN. MAMI WAS ALSO MY BIGGEST ROLE MODEL, MENTOR AND OUTSTANDING CHEER LEADER. MAMI'S WORDS OF WISDOM WERE "RESPECT OTHERS, BUT YOU MAKE SURE THEY RESPECT YOU". THERE WERE MORE WISE WORDS DURING MY GROWING UP, BUT THE RESPECT ONE PROVED ON POINT AGAIN AND AGAIN.

MAMI ARRIVED IN NEW YORK CITY IN 1949, FROM PUERTO RICO . LIFE IN PUERTO RICO FOR MAMI, DIDN'T ALLOWED MUCH SCHOOLING AND SHE WAS FARMED OUT TO HER OLDER SIBLINGS OR OTHER RELATIVES TO HELP THEM WITH ANYTHING THEY NEEDED. I LEARNED YEARS LATER THAT MAMI'S DAD WAS VERY BRUTAL WITH HER. THE LAST STRAW FOR HER WAS WHEN HER DAD WITNESSED A MALE TEACHER TALKING WITH AND SHOWING INTEREST IN MAMI. THOUGH SHE WAS AN ADULT HE STILL PHYSICALLY BEAT HER. THAT'S WHEN MAMI DECIDED TO LEAVE PUERTO RICO. I LEARNED THAT SHE DIDN'T TALK TO HIM UNTIL SEVERAL YEARS LATER. SHE MADE UP WITH HIM, BUT SHE DIDN'T FORGIVE HIM. I WAS AT HER HOSPITAL BEDSIDE WHEN SHE FORGAVE HIM AS SHE RECEIVED HER LAST RITES

ON THE 21ST OF DECEMBER 2017. SHE DIED ON DECEMBER 26, 2017. SHE IS NOW MY ANGEL.

MAMI WAS ASSISTED ON HER MOVE TO NEW YORK CITY BY AN AUNT NAMED ANNA. SHE RESIDED WITH SEVERAL OTHERS IN ANNA'S HOME IN THE BRONX. MAMI TOLD ME THAT THE LADY WAS NOT VERY PLEASANT, AND THAT SHE PAID ANNA $12.00 DOLLARS A WEEK, FOR PAYING HER PLANE FARE TO NEW YORK CITY. SHE FINISHED PAYING ANNA IN 1955. ANNA ALSO CHARGED MAMI FOR MEALS IF SHE ATE IN HER HOME. HOWEVER, IN FAIRNESS TO ANNA, SHE DID FACILITATE MAMI'S MOVE TO NEW YORK CITY.

MAMI FOUND EMPLOYMENT AT A GARMENT FACTORY LOCATED AT 625 BROADWAY WHERE SHE WORKED AS A SEAMSTRESS FOR TEN YEARS AND WAS PAID .79¢ AN HOUR. THE HOURS WERE 9:00 AM-5:00 PM AND HER BOSS WAS A MAN NAMED LEO. IT WAS DURING THIS TIME WHILE WORKING AT THE FACTORY WHERE SHE DEVELOPED LIFELONG FRIENDS WHO WOULD BE LIKE FAMILY FOR HER.

SHE MOVED OUT OF ANNA'S HOME AND LIVED IN DIFFERENT APARTMENTS IN MANHATTAN, INCLUDING AN APARTMENT SHE SHARED WITH HER SISTER AMPARO. I VISITED WITH TIA AMPARO IN 2006, AND TIA TOLD ME THAT SHE RETURNED TO PUERTO RICO BECAUSE THE COLD WEATHER HAD GOTTEN HER VERY ILL. I KNOW MAMI ALSO HAD ILLNESSES DUE TO THE COLD, BUT WHEN I ASKED MAMI WHY SHE STAYED IN NEW YORK, SHE RESPONDED THAT SHE LOVED NEW YORK. SHE LOVED NEW YORK CITY UNTIL HER LAST BREATH.

MY DAD WAS JOSE GABRIEL ORTIZ, BORN IN BARRANQUITA, PUERTO RICO. I DON'T KNOW MUCH ELSE ABOUT MY DAD. IN THE SUMMER OF 1968, MAMI TOOK ME TO PUERTO RICO AND INTRODUCED ME TO MY FATHER. SHE WAS ADAMANT ABOUT ME MEETING HIM AND GETTING TO KNOW HIM. THE MEETING WAS PLEASANT, BUT NOT

EMOTIONAL. I GOT TO MEET MY GRANDMA (DAD'S MOM) WHO WAS ALREADY IN THE LATE STAGES OF ALZHEIMER. MAMI SENT ME AGAIN THE FOLLOWING SUMMER FOR TWO WEEKS, WITH THE HOPES OF MY DAD AND I GETTING TO KNOW EACH OTHER A LITTLE BETTER. HOWEVER, THAT DIDN'T GO VERY WELL. IF HE SAID BLUE, I SAID BLACK AND VICE VERSA. I DID MEET HIM A FEW MORE TIMES AS I GOT OLDER, BUT WE NEVER DID HAVE A RELATIONSHIP. I WAS TOLD BY MAMI THAT HE LEFT BEFORE I WAS BORN AND SHOWED UP WHEN I WAS A YEAR OLD.

I STARTED WORKING ON MY FAMILY TREE, AND DISCOVERED THAT HE DIED ON AUGUST 28, 2002, AT THE AGE OF 69. I HAVE FORGIVEN HIM FOR NOT BEING THERE, BECAUSE I DON'T KNOW WHAT KIND OF LIFE HE HAD THAT MADE HIM THE FATHER HE WASN'T. I ALSO FOUND YEARS AGO THAT HE HAD A DAUGHTER NAMED YSENIA. I WAS ABLE TO MEET HER AND WE STAYED IN TOUCH FOR A WHILE, BUT EVENTUALLY WE LOST CONTACT. IT'S FUNNY BECAUSE I AM MEETING ALL KINDS OF 2ND,3RD,4TH, 5TH AND MORE COUSINS FROM MY DADS' SIDE THROUGH DNA ON ANCESTRY. I WISH I HAD BEEN SMART ENOUGH TO ASK QUESTIONS WHEN I MET HIS SIBLINGS, BUT I DIDN'T AND THEY ARE ALL GONE.

MY SISTERS' DAD WAS ANGEL. WE LIVED WITH ANGEL ON THE 5TH FLOOR OF 547 WEST 142 STREET, NEW YORK, AND LIVED THERE FROM 1957 - 1960, AND THEN THEY SEPARATED. I DON'T KNOW MUCH ABOUT HIM EITHER, BUT I DO REMEMBER HIM VISITING MY SISTERS AT AN APARTMENT WHERE MY MOM WAS RENTING A ROOM ON THE 6TH FLOOR, FROM A LADY NAMED DONA ANA. THE BUILDING WAS LOCATED AT 601 W. BROADWAY. THE LADY'S HUSBAND WAS A MERCHANT MARINE, SO SHE WAS ALWAYS ALONE. I REMEMBER STANDING NEXT TO MAMI WHEN SHE RECEIVED A CALL INFORMING HER THAT ANGEL HAD PASSED OF A HEART ATTACK. SHE STARTED TO CRY AND THEN FINDS OUT AT THE FUNERAL PARLOR THAT HE HAD ANOTHER FAMILY! HE DIED ON THE 17TH OF OCTOBER 1962, AT THE

AGE OF 30. MAMI DIDN'T DO WELL WITH THE MEN SHE PICKED, SO SHE DECIDED TO STAY ALONE EVEN THOUGH WE WOULD SUGGEST TO HER THAT SHE MEET SOMEONE. HER COMMENT WAS ALWAYS "I DON'T NEED ANYONE AND I WILL NOT BRING ANYONE HERE WHO IS GOING TO HURT MY KIDS". MY MOM WAS VERY BEAUTIFUL, PETIT, LOVING AND TOUGH.

I WAS TAKEN CARE OF BY A LADY NAMED MITA, WHILE MAMI WORKED, AND I SPENT A LOT OF TIME WITH MITA, MANY TIMES NOT SURE OF MAMI'S OR MY SISTER'S WHEREABOUTS. THAT MYSTERY WAS SOLVED AFTER I WAS MUCH OLDER WHEN MAMI EXPLAINED THAT MY SISTERS WERE BEING TAKEN CARE OF BY A LADY NAMED "TATA", ON THE 2ND FLOOR OF THE 601 W. BROADWAY BUILDING. MITA WAS A CHARACTER THAT I STILL REMEMBER TODAY. SHE WAS A VERY STRONG BRUNETTE WHO RULED WITH AN IRON HAND. I REMEMBER GOING WITH HER TO A LITTLE AREA WITH BENCHES IN THE MIDDLE OF BROADWAY BLVD. SHE WOULD SIT AND WATCH A HARDWARE STORE BETWEEN 141 STREET AND 142 STREET. A MAN WORKING THERE WOULD SPOT HER, COME OVER AND TALK WITH HER. HE WOULD SHOW UP LATER AT HER APARTMENT AND THEY WOULD GET IT ON. I REMEMBER HER PUTTING ME IN A BEDROOM AND TELLING ME TO STAY AND NOT TO COME OUT UNTIL SHE TOLD ME TO COME OUT. HOWEVER, I DID LEAVE THE ROOM A FEW TIMES AND I COULD HEAR SOME NOISES COMING OUT OF HER BEDROOM. I FINALLY UNDERSTOOD AS I GOT MUCH OLDER THAT THEY WERE GETTING IT ON. I WAS ONLY 6 YEARS OLD, SO WHAT DID I KNOW, LOL.

I WAS LIVING WITH MITA WHEN I ATTENDED FIRST AND SECOND GRADES AT OUR LADY OF LOURDES CATHOLIC SCHOOL. IT'S ALSO WHERE I DID MY COMMUNION AND CONFIRMATION. I REMEMBER ONE DAY RETURNING TO MITA'S AFTER I GOT OUT OF SCHOOL. I ENTERED THE BUILDING AND THERE WAS THIS MAN WHO SAID HELLO AND THEN HANDED ME A NICKEL. I TOOK THE NICKEL AND WHEN I LOOKED UP, THE MAN WAS PLAYING WITH HIMSELF! I SCREAMED

AND THREW THE NICKEL AT HIM AND RAN UP ONE FLIGHT OF STAIRS TO MITA'S.

I TOLD MITA WHAT HAD HAPPENED AND SHE GRABBED A KNIFE AND WENT LOOKING FOR HIM. I AM GLAD SHE DIDN'T FIND HIM, BECAUSE SHE WOULD HAVE CUT OFF HIS PECKER. ONE OF THE MEMORIES THAT I HAVE OF OUR LADY OF LOURDES WAS BEING TAUGHT TO PLAY THE PIANO BY A NUN. ONE OF HER TECHNIQUES IN TEACHING WAS TO HIT MY KNUCKLES EVERY TIME I PLAYED A WRONG NOTE. I FINALLY BEGGED MY MOTHER TO STOP SENDING ME TO PIANO LESSONS. I REGRET NOT LEARNING, BUT I'LL TALK ABOUT OTHER NUN STORIES AS I GO ALONG.

MITA ALSO TOOK CARE OF A COUPLE OTHER KIDS. ONE WAS A BIT ON THE NUTTY SIDE. I REMEMBER HIM THROWING HIS RABBIT AGAINST A RADIATOR, AND KILLING THE RABBIT INSTANTLY. I DON'T KNOW WHAT HAPPENED TO THE KID BECAUSE MITA TOLD THE MOM THAT SHE DIDN'T WANT HIM AROUND ANYMORE. SHE ALSO TOOK CARE OF A GIRL ABOUT MY AGE. THE RELATIONSHIP BETWEEN MAMI AND MITA CAME TO A QUICK END ONE DAY. MITA HAD THIS CRAZY IDEA THAT SHE WOULD TAKE CUSTODY OF ME BECAUSE I WAS SPENDING SO MUCH TIME IN HER CARE. MAMI GOT VERY UPSET AND TOLD HER THAT WAS NOT GOING TO HAPPEN. I NEVER SAW MITA AGAIN AND MAMI STOPPED WORKING. OUR MOM GAVE UP ANY DREAMS SHE HAD FOR HERSELF AT THAT MOMENT AND JUST CONCENTRATED ON RAISING HER THREE CHILDREN, SAFELY WITHOUT ANY CHANCES OF LOSING US. I ALWAYS WONDERED WHY MAMI CHOSE TO STOP GOING FOR ANY DREAMS SHE HAD, BUT I GUESS THAT BEING A MOM AND RAISING US WAS HER MOST IMPORTANT GOAL.

IT WAS MEMORABLE WHEN MAMI TOOK US TO THE PARK AT RIVERSIDE DRIVE, AT 142 STREET. AS WE REACHED THE PARK. MAMI WOULD GET A THIN BRANCH FROM A TREE, CLEAN THE LEAVES OFF IT AND SHOW IT TO US. SHE WOULD SAY TO US "LA VEN, OLENLA, QUE

YOU NO TENGA QUE USARLA". THE TRANSLATION IS "YOU SMELL IT, DON'T MAKE ME USE IT". SO NEEDLESS TO SAY WE WERE THE BEST BEHAVED KIDS IN THE PARK. WE WERE UNDER THE SAME WARNING WHEN WOULD VISIT PEOPLE. THEY WOULD COMPLEMENT MAMI FOR HAVING SUCH WELL BEHAVED KIDS. LITTLE DID THEY KNOW THAT WE WERE UNDER A WARNING.

ONE OF MY ADVENTURES AS A KID LIVING IN MANHATTAN WAS WHEN I AND ANOTHER FRIEND DECIDED TO FOLLOW A FRIEND AND HIS FRIENDS. THEY WARNED US TO STAY BACK, BUT WE FOLLOWED FOR A BIT AND THEN LOSE THEM OR THEY LOST US. THE TWO OF US CONTINUE TO PLAY AT RIVERSIDE PARK, INCLUDING ON THE TRACKS THAT WERE BELOW THE PARK. WE PLAYED UNTIL IT GOT DARK AND THEN I FOLLOWED MY FRIEND HOME. I TOLD MY FRIEND'S MOM THAT I KNEW HOW TO GET HOME AND WALKED HOME ALONE. LITTLE DID I KNOW THAT THE MOM FOLLOWED ME. MAMI WAS WORRIED OUT OF HER MIND AND HAD CALLED THE COPS. WHEN I GOT HOME, I GOT LOTS OF KISSES, HUGS AND A WARNING THAT I WAS GOING TO PAY FOR WHAT I DID TO HER, BUT NOT THAT NIGHT. IT DIDN'T TAKE LONG TO GET THE SPANKING I HAD COMING, LOL.

I REMEMBER OUR LIVING IN MANHATTAN AS A TIME WHERE WE HAD PEOPLE THAT WE LOVED AND LOVED US. PEOPLE LIKE "YAYA" AND HER DAUGHTER PEGGY, MECHE (FAMILY TO MY SISTERS DAD) AND "TATA", BUT WE HAD NO PLACE OF OUR OWN. THEN IN 1963, MY UNCLE BENJAMIN (RIP) HELPED MAMI FIND AN APARTMENT. WE MOVED TO 456 E. 175 STREET, APARTMENT 3A, LOCATED AT 175 STREET, BETWEEN PARK AND WASHINGTON AVENUE IN THE BRONX. WE FINALLY HAD A HOME OF OUR OWN.

I FOUND OUT YEARS LATER THAT MAMI HATED THE BRONX AND HATED LEAVING ALL HER FRIENDS. WE VISITED THOSE OLD FRIENDS AND NEIGHBORHOOD EVERY WEEK AND CONTINUED UNTIL WE

WERE A LOT OLDER. I THINK OF THEM ALL AND WONDER WHERE EVERYBODY IS OR HAVE THEY LEFT US?

ONE THING THAT LEFT A BIG IMPRESSION ON ME, WHEN I WAS ATTENDING THE SECOND GRADE AT OUR LADY OF LOURDES SCHOOL, ON AMSTERDAM AND 142 STREET. I SAW A FRIEND TRYING TO CATCH UP TO US AND RUNNING ACROSS THE STREET, WHERE HE WAS HIT BY A TRUCK. I STILL REMEMBER HIM GETTING HIT, BEING ROLLED UNDER THE TRUCK. THE DRIVER STOPPED AND WENT TO THE REAR OF HIS TRUCK TO CHECK MY FRIEND. I DON'T THINK HE DIED AT THE SCENE, BUT I AM NOT SURE AND I NEVER SAW MY FRIEND AGAIN.

CHAPTER 2

THE APARTMENT WAS A LARGE THREE BEDROOM. IT HAD A LIVING ROOM, BATHROOM AND KITCHEN. WOW, WE WERE MOVING ON UP, AT LEASE FOR A SHORT WHILE. MY UNCLE BENJAMIN, HIS WIFE TIA ANGELICA, AND HIS CHILDREN EVELYN, BENNY JR. AND LILLIAN LIVED ABOVE US IN APARTMENT 4A. MY UNCLE WILLIE AND HIS FAMILY MOVED OUT OF 450 E. 175 ST, WHICH WAS THE BUILDING NEXT DOOR, AND MY AUNT MARY MOVED IN WITH CARLOS AND HER CHILDREN VIVIAN, ANGEL AND ERIC. I HAD MY OWN BEDROOM, THE GIRLS SHARED A BEDROOM AND MAMI TOOK THE SMALLER BEDROOM. WE WENT FROM NOT HAVING ANY FAMILY, TO ALL OF A SUDDEN HAVING NINE COUSINS ALL AT ONCE! HOWEVER, AFTER A FEW YEARS THE OTHER FAMILIES STARTED TO DO WELL FINANCIALLY AND MOVED TO OTHER LOCATIONS. HOWEVER, WE ENJOYED OUR FAMILY AND THE NEW NEIGHBORS. TO THIS DAY WE KEEP IN TOUCH WITH OUR COUSINS. ONE OF MY NEPHEWS IS AMAZED AND WONDERS HOW WHEN WE GET TOGETHER. IT SEEMS AS IF WE HAD NEVER MOVED AWAY FROM EACH OTHER. WE JUST GREW UP CLOSE TO EACH OTHER. TODAY I STILL CALL MY AUNTS AND COUSINS JUST TO SAY I LOVE THEM.

OUR NEIGHBORHOOD WAS A MIXTURE OF ITALIANS, IRISH, PUERTO RICANS, ECUADORIANS AND OTHER HISPANICS. EVENTUALLY THE ITALIANS AND IRISH MOVED OUT. YOU LEARNED AT AN EARLY AGE THAT AS YOUR ECONOMIC POSITION IMPROVES YOU MOVED ON UP

OR AT LEAST OUT OF THE HOOD, PLUS MOST PEOPLE WANT TO LIVE CLOSE TO THEIR OWN KIND. My story is not a new story. I was raised by a single mom, in a household with very little money and yes, welfare helped us. However, Mami accomplished a lot and we never went hungry, we were always well dressed, and the most important part is that we were all successful and never continued the cycle of welfare dependency. So I learned from mami that there is no excuse for not trying to improve yourself and reaching your dreams. You can't blame others or anything for not making it. Another of Mami's teachings.

I had some memorable friends. First there was Alfred. He was a black kid who lived in the building on the NE corner of 175 street and Washington Avenue. The apartment was above a small store. I remember Alfred and I playing Batman and Robin. I was Robin and Alfred was Batman. I only have a few memories of us playing. I think we were eight years old. I don't remember when Alfred moved or why, but I remember Batman. I believe that's why I was always comfortable with Blacks. I wish when I was young that I had the presence of mind to at least ask Alfred his last name.

Some of my childhood friends have left this life, but I remember Barney, Joey, Willie, Ralphie, Juan, Pablo, Nelson and Rodney. As we know, life goes on and it goes by quickly. Some of these friends I found along the way and some have passed away. I remember them all fondly. We really didn't have any bad ones, though I know one died because of drug use. Our growing up wasn't complicated, though drugs and gangs were real. We had colorful gangs with names like, the Ghetto Brothers, the Savage Skulls, The Royal Javelins, etc. They were dangerous, but the all out use of firearms was still many years away. These gang bangers carried knives (007), wore Levi jackets with their colors displayed on their backs. The movie "The Warriors", in 1979, showed these types of gangs and colors. However, they never got any members from my block. I don't know why that happened, but I remember one day a few walking down our block and all the men in the buildings came out. They walked by quietly and didn't bother anyone, lol. Brave, no? We did have a kid in the building across the street who was robbing an apartment with a couple of his friends. They killed the man who lived in the apartment, when he walked in and surprised them. They were trying to get things to steal and sell for their drug purchases.

When we first moved into apartment 3A, it was big and comfortable. Mami made a great home for us. Then the landlord allowed the building to go to shit. It wasn't just our landlord, but a lot of owners in our area. We learned that the buildings were better off vacant, then with tenants who didn't always pay the rent on time. In 1973, the term "The Bronx is burning" could be heard again and again. We never had enough heat or hot water. Mami would heat up large pots of water on the stove then carry them to the bathtub. She would fill the tub and we would take turns taking what she called "cat baths". One day as she approached the bathroom with a pot of scalding water, my sister who was hiding behind the bathroom door, ran into Mami and the water fell right onto her causing a bad burn.

I believe she still feels the cold of that apartment. We used tons of blankets and layers of clothing to stay warm. There was also a hole in the bathroom ceiling, around the radiator that was never repaired. In January of 1980, I took my future wife Rosemary to meet my mom and sisters. We stayed in that apartment for a few days and finally were invited to stay with my Tia Carmin. Rosemary couldn't believe what we had to endure. I remember on the first night Rosemary wearing a thin night gown and my mom asking her if she was sure that she would feel warm. That night we covered ourselves with several blankets, lol. It was my way of welcoming her to the Bronx. My sisters were able to move Mami out of that building in 1981 and into 2323 Cambreleng Avenue.

WHEN WE MOVED TO THE BRONX IN 1963, MAMI ENROLLED US IN ST. JOSEPH'S CATHOLIC SCHOOL ON BATHGATE AVENUE, BETWEEN TREMONT AVENUE AND 177 STREET. I REMEMBER THAT THIS WAS THE FIRST TIME IN MY LIFE WHEN YOU REMEMBER WHERE YOU WERE WHEN SOMETHING BIG HAPPENS. I REMEMBER BEING IN THE THIRD GRADE AND WE WERE WATCHING A MOVIE IN THE CHURCH HALL. THE MOVIE WAS INTERRUPTED AND THE PRINCIPLE (SISTER ANITA) TOLD US TO GO HOME. WHEN I GOT HOME I FOUND MAMI CRYING IN FRONT OF THE TELEVISION. IT WAS THE DAY THAT JOHN F. KENNEDY WAS ASSASSINATED.

IT'S BEEN SAID THAT WAS THE MOMENT OUR COUNTRY LOST ITS' INNOCENCE. WE WERE CLUED TO THE TELEVISION AS WE WATCHED THE FUNERAL FOR PRESIDENT KENNEDY. OUR FIRST TEACHERS AT ST. JOSEPHS' WERE CALLED BROTHERS AND THEN NUNS TOOK OVER. I DIDN'T CARE FOR EITHER ONE OF THEM BECAUSE THEY WERE PHYSICALLY BRUTAL. I ALWAYS TELL THE STORY THAT IF I SHOULD EVER RUN INTO A CERTAIN NUN WHO BEAT ME BECAUSE I DIDN'T DO MY HOMEWORK, I WILL BEAT HER ASS LIKE SHE BEAT ME. I THINK IT'S SAFE TO ASSUME THAT SHE'S WITH OUR MAKER.

THE BLOCK WHERE THE SCHOOL AND CHURCH WERE LOCATED ALSO PLAYED A BIG PART IN MY LIFE'S DREAMS. THE 48TH POLICE PRECINCT WAS LOCATED NEXT TO THE CHURCH ON BATHGATE AVENUE. I WOULD SIT AND WATCH POLICE OFFICERS BRING IN PRISONERS AND TAKE THEM INTO THE BUILDING FOR PROCESSING. I WOULD CHAT NOW AND THEN WITH OFFICERS WHO TOOK TIME OUT TO SIT ON THE PRECINCT STOOP AND CHAT WITH ME. IT LEFT A BIG IMPRESSION WITH ME. A FEW YEARS LATER THE PRECINCT WAS MOVED BETWEEN WASHINGTON AVENUE AND PARK AVENUE, BEHIND OUR BLOCK! I GOT TO KNOW ONE OF MY ROLE MODEL, OUR BEAT COP SAM. A NICE IRISH COP WHO KNEW US ALL. HE PLAYED STICK BALL WITH US IN FRONT OF THE FIREHOUSE ON 176 STREET, BETWEEN PARK AND WASHINGTON AVENUE, AND WOULD ALWAYS TAKE TIME TO

TALK WITH US. WHEN I GOT MY ACCEPTANCE LETTER FROM THE U.S. BORDER PATROL, I WENT INTO THE 48 PRECINCT AND FOUND SAM, NOW A SERGEANT WORKING THE DESK. I SHOWED HIM THE LETTER AND HE CONGRATULATED ME. WHEN I TOLD HIM THAT HE WAS MY INSPIRATION FOR GETTING INTO LAW ENFORCEMENT, HE TURNED RED AND THANKED ME. I TRIED A COUPLE OF YEARS AGO TO IDENTIFY SAM'S LAST NAME, BUT I WAS NOT SUCCESSFUL. IF SOMEONE READING THIS KNOWS WHO SAM IS OR WAS, THANK HIM FOR ME.

ANOTHER COP WHO WAS A ROLE MODEL WAS OFFICER CASTRO FROM THE SAME PRECINCT. HE WAS THE COP WHO RESPONDED WHEN I AND A FRIEND ENDED UP FIGHTING MEMBERS OF A STREET GANG NAMED THE "SAVAGE SKULLS". SEVERAL OF THEIR MEMBERS WERE BEATING UP ON A WHITE KID AT OUR BUS STOP. MY FRIEND AND I JUMPED IN AND RESCUED THE WHITE KID, BUT I ENDED FIGHTING AND BEING ASSAULTED BY SOME OF THE GANG MEMBERS AND GETTING A CUT ON MY HEAD WHEN ONE OF THEM HIT ME WITH THE BUTT OF A KNIFE. LUCKILY HE DIDN'T STAB ME WITH IT. WHEN THE COPS SHOWED UP THE GANG MEMBERS RAN OFF AND I WAS HEADED HOME. OFFICER CASTRO SCOLDED ME, AND TOLD ME THAT IF I WAS BRAVE ENOUGH TO STAND UP FOR THE KID, THEN I SHOULD BE BRAVE ENOUGH TO FOLLOW THROUGH ON THE IDIOTS THAT WE FOUGHT. WE FOUND SOME OF THEM, I TESTIFIED IN COURT AND THEY GOT SOME JAIL TIME, BUT GOING BACK TO THE STORY. I GOT HOME AND MAMI GOT SCARED. MY WHITE CLINTON HIGH SCHOOL LETTER JACKET WAS COVERED IN BLOOD FROM MY HEAD WOUND. SHE TOOK ME TO THE HOSPITAL AND I ENDED UP GETTING FOUR STITCHES. OFFICER CASTRO LOOKED IN ON ME A FEW TIMES. THANKS OFFICER CASTRO. I WISH I CAN FIND YOU AND THANK YOU FOR BEING ANOTHER ONE OF MY ROLE MODELS. ONE DAY THE MOTHER OF ONE OF THE GANG BANGERS CAME TO THE PHARMACY I WORKED IN. SHE LOOKED AT ME AND ASKED ME MY NAME. I GAVE HER A FICTITIOUS NAME AND SHE BOUGHT IT AND LEFT. I THOUGHT

SHE MIGHT REMEMBER ME, BUT I NEVER SAW HER OR HER SON AGAIN. I LEARNED FROM THAT EXPERIENCE TO FOLLOW THROUGH WITH WHAT I STARTED IN DEFENDING MYSELF OR OTHERS.

I CARRY THAT PHILOSOPHY TODAY AND ALWAYS HAVE. ANOTHER THING THAT HAPPENED WAS THAT I MADE A CHANGE OF FRIENDS THE DAY AFTER I HELPED THAT KID AND GOT INJURED. I ARRIVED EARLY THE NEXT MORNING TO THE HOUSE WHERE WE WOULD MEET OUTSIDE AND HANG. THE FRIENDS WHO GOT ON THE BUS AND LEFT ME AND EDWIN WERE GATHERED THERE. I WAS A BIT PISSED, WHEN I ASKED THEM TO EXPLAIN WHY THEY DID NOT HELP US? ONE OF THEM SAID THAT IT WASN'T OUR BUSINESS, BUT AT LEAST THEY TOOK CARE OF MY BOOK BAG. THAT WAS THE LAST TIME I HUNG OUT WITH THAT GROUP OF SO CALLED FRIENDS. IT HAS ALWAYS BEEN IMPORTANT FOR ME TO HELP SOMEONE, EVEN IF IT MEANS HAVING TO DEFEND MYSELF.

Mami was able to send us to catholic school from third grade to eight grade and on some summers she would set aside airline tickets to Puerto Rico and pay them on layaway and we would visit our grandparents. I also remember her buying an encyclopedia on layaway. She kept us busy with the Sea Cadets, Karate and dance. I helped with the expense for karate and the Sea Cadets because I was working for my uncle Benny and then at a pharmacy on Tremont Avenue.

I don't remember a time when mami treated herself to something nice. Once the summer had ended and we returned to school, the teachers (nuns) would ask us about our summer vacation. Being embarrassed about being a welfare kid and not going anywhere most summers, I would lie about our summer vacation. It wasn't until a comment was made by one of those nun's that made me feel proud of Mami and us. Mami also knew how to do lay away on trips that we took or where she sent us to Puerto Rico. She did so much, with so little.

The nun stated that Puerto Ricans were born, raised and would die in the same place. I felt bad and pissed off by the comment. I knew at that moment that Mami raised us to go out and make something of ourselves. I also learned as I got older and moved around that you could always find a Puerto Rico or Dominican everywhere. So much for the nun's comment. I was never ashamed again of mami, our economic status or my ethnic blood. I learned that even religious folks were bigoted or just naive. I was involved with St. Joseph's church for many years. However, I started having mixed feelings about nuns, priests and the church itself.

Mami believed in discipline, which today would have landed her in trouble, but I am glad she kept us on a tight leash. She was always complimented on how well behaved the three of us were, with friends not knowing that we were warned ahead of time what the consequences would be if we didn't behave. I didn't laugh about it then, but today I am glad she raised us the way she did. I never thought of my mom as brutal, but as I got to know her siblings, I found that Mami had been brutalized by her dad and older sisters while growing up and that's what she learned and applied on us. I also remember my younger sister telling me that she thought mami was brutal with her and her sister, but they still stepped up and always took care of mami. That was a different time, with different ideas, and barbaric ways. However, Mami always came to us after she hit us and explained why she hit us and always said she loved us. Maybe it was that tough love that kept us away from the gangs in the area, the heroin addiction taking hold of some of our neighbors, and my sisters and I from being parents at a young age. The cross Bronx Expressway was located behind our block. Traffic got off the Third Avenue exit, followed 175 street, pass our block and then at Webster Avenue, travelers could gas up and then get back on the expressway.

Mami and I spent countless hours resting on our elbows at our window sill and watching the traffic. We saw many different license tags and we talked about where the people were from and wondered where they were headed. This is the time that we spoke about life, the future and our dreams. When I was nine years old, I was leaning on that window sill with mami, when we watched two cops go into our building and come out with an individual. They put him in the back of the squad car and drove off. I mentioned to Mami that I wanted to be a cop. She told me that it was a dangerous job, but if I was going to do it, to be good, respectful with people and do my job right. She had given me her blessings. I pursued that dream by taking several exams. One exam took me to Portland, Maine! A guy named Steve was stationed with me at Parris Island, South Carolina, Marine Corps Training. He remembered that I wanted to be a cop and put in an application for the exam in my name.

I applied for the test, went up, took the test and hung out with Steve. I never got the job, but it was nice to see that he remembered. I've tried looking him up on Facebook, but haven't located him. On November 6, 1978, I was hired by the United States Border Patrol. I will discuss my time and career with the United States Border Patrol, but right now let's go back to the Bronx.

My neighborhood was usually pretty safe, but there were signs of changes taking place. First, we had some guys who had returned from Vietnam in sad shape. These individuals lived in our neighborhood and selected our building as the place to prepare and use their heroin. Mami would send me to the store and I would have to slide pass these guys as they cooked their drug at the bottom step of our stairwell. Then on my return from the store they would be nodding out behind the stairwell. It might have been this sight that could have persuaded me not to use or try drugs. There was nothing beautiful about three guys nodding out, oblivious to what or who was going around them.

Overall my memories of my neighborhood were great! The street games like tag, ringo livio, Johnny on the Pony. Friends like Pablo, Nelson, "Tutu", my cousin Benny Jr and some of the pretty girls. Today my friend Sergio and I still stay in contact and we talk on the phone now and then. I remember many of my old neighborhood friends fondly. I have also found some of my wrestling team mates and coach on Facebook, which makes it a great way to catch up and share some memories. I found Pablo's wife through facebook and stay in touch with her. I get sentimental during the Christmas holiday season and reach out to friends and family. I guess I learned from mami to value good friends. We had little money, but I never missed anything, thanks to mami. Yes, she was a role model and she stayed with us a lot. However, she refused to move with us because she always missed New York. One of my favorite pastimes was when I would close myself in my room, take my small portable record player and listen and sing to the 45s I was given by Peggy. I think that's one of the things that drove me to sing.

I started working when I was about 12 for another role model. Mami's brother Tio Benjamin (RIP) and his wife Angelica (RIP). He bought their first grocery store (bodega) on Washington Avenue, a bit north of the corner of 175 street, facing Washington, Avenue. I learned some of my work ethics from him and Tia Angelica. My aunt was a very loving, strong, but stern woman.

However, before he got his own business, he worked in a bakery. I remember him dropping off some bread at our apartment when he got home from work. A few years later he sold that bodega and bought another one half a block up from his first one. This store was bigger and he had a steady clientele of firemen. He sold lots of food and beer to these firemen. There was a large freezer in the back room of the bodega where he kept lots of quart size beer bottles of Miller, Reingold and Valentine ale. This was an extra freezer because he also stored these beers for the regular customers in the front of the store. One day a customer came in and asked for a quart of beer which I didn't have in the front freezer, so I went to the back and got the bottle of beer.

My uncle was smiling, but seemed pissed. As soon as the customer left he started to scold me, letting me know that the beer in the back freezer was strictly for the fireman! I apologized and never did that again.

He also scolded me when he caught me eating some cookies. He ask me "what would he sell if I kept eating his inventory", lol. However, he would allow me to eat something of my choosing, like a few slim Jims with a pepsi or some pepperoni with crackers and Pepsi. I had a great diet back then, lol. My uncle did really well in the bodega business and was the first one to leave the Bronx, moving to Long Island, buying a house and raising his kids. I have always idolized him and Tia for being the wonderful people they were. He was also great with his sister (my mom). We lost him in 2017, two months before mami. I have pictures of him with mami, and other siblings. Another thing he had was a great sense of humor. I stayed with him one time at his house in Long Island and I am glad I did, because he passed not long after. What an amazing man.

The second to leave the Bronx was Tio Willie and his family. They moved to Puerto Rico first, but after a year they returned to the Bronx. My uncle owned a very busy and successful barbershop where I worked on Saturdays and summers. He was quite a character and was always well dressed, with lots of bucks in his pocket. I found through the years that he was more of a wise guy, but he was good to Mami and us. His son Willito, took care of his dad until the end. He died in 2016.

The last one to move was my Tia Mary and Carlos. They moved to the Castle Hill area of the Bronx. It was nicer and more upscale.

Then they moved to New Jersey where Carlos still runs a successful business. Carlos married my aunt Mary and gave his last name to his adopted children. He also gave them a lively hood and continued with their children. He is also my role model. I've always tried keeping in touch with him and aunt Mary. He has made careers for all his kids and a few grandkids.

Mami kept us active so we didn't have the time to hang out and get into trouble. She signed me up for a program called the "Sea Cadets", which was a military type of organization that taught youngsters to drill, take orders and we used Navy uniforms. I made it to Petty Officer.

In 1969, I learned a lesson about bullying and bigger fish. I picked on a kid who lived across the street from my Tio Benny's store. He walked away and a big older guy showed up and I used my face to block his amazing fast and accurate fists. I was able to pick him up and throw him on the ground, but the fight was stopped by my Tio Benny! I went home and knocked on my door and mami answered. She saw my face and screamed "Ay mijo, que paso?" I told her what happened and being the smart women she always was, she took me the next day and signed me up for karate classes. She told me "if you are going to fight, learn how to fight". I was working so I paid for the classes. It's funny how things work out. Once I started studying karate, I never got into any fights? Crazy, no? However, I never bullied anyone again and I always remembered the story of the bigger fish, lol.

Our block consisted of our building (456) and (450) to the left of us, plus four private homes, to the left of (450). Across the street was another apartment building, with a burial monument store on the corner to the left of the building and a warehouse to the right. Across Park Avenue, there was a Salvation Army building, and train tracks ran the length of Park Avenue. You could walk down going west on

175 street, down to Webster Avenue, where we would go and buy some White Castle hamburgers for eighteen cents. If you walked east on 175 street, you would get to Crotona Park.

I returned to the neighborhood years after I left, and realized that my world wasn't very big, but it was a good one. Now everything is gone, with the exception of the private homes. I could see bad and good from my window.

CHAPTER 3

We spent a lot of time in Crotona Park and it was lots of fun when we had snow. Our friend Ray had a sled and we would ride that sled down this big hill. There was no fence and luckily we never crossed onto Third Avenue. On one such day Ray was riding down the hill and flew up and landed hard. He took off running, and left his sled. We picked up his sled and went to his house. We found out that when he landed on the sled, a protruding nail cut a nice piece of skin off his ass. That was the end of our sled rides. Ray and his family moved out of the neighborhood. His family and one more left the neighborhood.

My friends and I were members of the CYO (Catholic Youth Organization) and played on a softball team. One day our team participated in a game in Van Cortland Park with another team from another church. The other team members was mostly white and during the game some older guys started calling me a spic. I would answer back and tell then I was Superspic. Once the game was finished, we started walking towards the bus stop. We were stopped by the guy who was the main instigator, and surrounded by his friends. Our backs were to the park building housing the restrooms. The main instigator kept pushing me towards the door of a restroom. I knew once he got me inside, I would be in trouble. I had the catcher's mask in my hand and when he went to push me I hit him in the face with the metal part of the mask. Luckily the cops were rushing toward us and the punks ran away. Thankfully, one of the folks with the other team must have talked to the police about our predicament.

I've got several good memories of my time with the CYO (Catholic Youth Organization). The one that stands out was when we had seen a special by News reporter Geraldo Rivera in 1972, about the Willowbrook State Hospital, in Staten Island. It was a very sad and horrible look at how mentally challenged children and adults were neglected in the institution. So we decided to collect toys and clothes and take a trip to Willowbrook and spend some time with these children. There was a good group of us, including my sister Sonia. The ride on the subway was buzzing with happiness, excitement for the task we were going to do.

However, when we got to Willowbrook and we were pretty much told that our effort was an honorable idea, but we couldn't give the children the toys we had brought with us. We saw firsthand what a hard task it would be. The staff told us that we could not give out the toys because the children would hurt each other with the toys. So we left with everything we brought with us. The ride back was very quiet, sad and everyone of us was in shock.

We spent most of our time playing softball at the P.S.58 school yard, stickball, touch football and just hanged out at the school yard. Once in a while the black kids from Bathgate would come to the school yard and we would play softball against them. We all got along and there was never any trouble between us. The school yard is where we drank Boons farm Apple Wine when we got into our teens. That was some cheap stuff, but it was all we could afford.

The public library on the corner of Washington Avenue and 176 street was another get away for me. I spent lots of hours reading books about horses, cowboys and police adventures. As I got older

I would do my homework there and hang with my friends in the library. We behaved so the librarians never had a reason to throw us out. It's funny how fast time goes. I think about those years and I relished my time in that hood.

After graduating from St. Joseph's, I decided I had enough of Catholic school and I asked my mom if I could attend a public high school. She agreed and I entered DeWitt Clinton High school from 1969-1973. It was an all boys public high school, with great athletic sports programs and history. It was at DeWitt Clinton where I met my biggest role model.

I was trying out for the football team one day and I wasn't really doing well. I was small and didn't weight much. The coach came up to me and started screaming that he needed me to stop before I got hurt. He told me to go back to the school and see what other type of team I could try out for.

So I walked in all bummed out and found the wrestling room. I stopped, looked in and was hooked. There was the coach working out his wrestlers. He saw me and came to ask me what was going on?

I told him about the football attempt and how the coach told me to find something else that I could participate in. Coach Robert Stahli told me without any hesitation, that I was welcomed to come wrestle. I started working out with the team, ended up a good wrestler and in 1973, took first place in my weight division. What stood out with coach Stahli, was his compassion, his caring and his talent and willingness to share it with his team, which was made up of some low income black, Hispanic and white boys. However, he also showed his humanity and his being a caring man by inviting and taking us to his home one summer for a bar-be-queue. We met his children, his wife and he made us feel at home. When I graduated from the Border Patrol Academy, I went home for a quick visit, which included visiting Coach Stahli. I found him in the gym and showed him my badge. I told him how I felt about him. I told him again in 2018, when I found him on Facebook!

I volunteered to be a hall monitor and was assigned to work the cafeteria. I was a stickler for rules and got into some push and shove matches. I think it was just another example of where I was headed in my life's work.

My friendship with the friends from 175 street changed one day when I and Edwin jumped in to help a kid that was being beat by members of the Savage Skulls. Those friends continued home and never helped us. The next day when I asked why they didn't jump in and help, they said that it was not any of their business and that I shouldn't have jumped in. I realized then that my values and the values of the supposed friends were different. Luckily they did take my book bag home with them and I got it back the next day when I spoke with them. Mami always said to me that an acquaintance was a dollar in the pocket, but a friend would always be there.

That was the last time I hung out with them. Many years later I reached out to one of them, but he soon passed away. I don't hold any hard feelings, but that lesson taught me what true friends are and I didn't have any true friends except for two. That was Carlos V, and Freddy P (R.I.P), both who were from Ecuador. I still talk to Carlos every now and then.

I applied for a job at a Pharmacy located on Tremont, between Third and Bathgate Avenue. Another kid had beat me to the job, but the next day the Pharmacist called my house and asked if I was still interested? I told him I was and he asked me to come in for an interview. When I was interviewed I was told that the reason the job was open again was that the kid who was hired before me was caught stealing money from the cash register. I stayed at the pharmacy for six years and was very loyal to them.

I worked for two pharmacists and co-owners who I will call Milton and Larry (not their real names). Larry was much more serious then Milton, but he was very honest and loved teaching us. A few years after I left the pharmacy, Larry called my house and offered me a chance to go to St. John's University and become a pharmacist. Then he said that once I finished, I would get a store and be part of their company. I think it may have been the beginnings of something like Walgreens or CVS. I thanked him, but informed Larry that I still wanted to be a cop. He called again a few years later and made the same offer. However, I declined again because I still wanted to get into law enforcement. It's funny how I always got along with the managers that were a little more serious and disciplined.

One of the memorable things I did as a senior and the beginning of college, was as a member of a group started by a local priest named "Nabori". The word meant "worker/warrior", a word from the Taino native of Puerto Rico. We would go to high schools with large minority students and give speeches that a few of us in the group wrote and would speak at these high schools. The schools were located in different Boros in NYC, Connecticut, New Jersey and Pennsylvania. My speech was named "Two Strikes, but only you Can Strike out". I remember after one of our presentations, a man coming to me and asking if I was going to be a politician"? I told him that I was going to be a cop and he told me I should think it over, lol. I did become a mentor and I used my only you can strike out again and again.

The reason I quit the pharmacy was because I joined the United States Marine Corps Reserves and left for boot camp on October 1975. I had been attending John Jay College of Criminal Justice, but after two years, my GPA was so bad that I was given a year off from school. One day while walking on Fordham Road and Grand Concourse I decided to walk into the Navy/Marine Corps recruiting station. I decided to join the Marine Corps Reserves. My training was in Parris Island, South Carolina, as a recruit in Platoon 383, on October 28, 1975. I know that I made a mistake not going in as an active Marine, but I found a job quickly and was later hired by the United States Border Patrol, so I stayed a reservist.

I always remember my mom trying to convince me to go and get my time over with. Once again, I feel it was the worst mistake I made. I just focused on being a cop somewhere, so I never made the move to go to the regulars.

My training as a Marine recruit in Parris Island was an experience that I will always treasure and credit as part of what made me who I am today. It was no frills and physically demanding. My three drill instructors were SSGT. Saunders, Sgt Moody and Sgt. Pridgeon. Each one memorable and colorful in their own way.

The two Sgts. were the crazy ones and SSGT. Saunders who was the lead drill instructor was a bit more serious, but not as crazy, unless you were stupid enough to get him riled up. I personally saw firsthand why the training had to be so mentally and physically demanding.

One night we were awakened by SSGT. Saunders screaming at us to get out of our racks! He approaches a recruit who was in one of the rear bunks and starts screaming at him "the next time you want to hang yourself, call me so you can achieve your goal". The recruit had tied a sheet from the top bunk to the floor and tried hanging himself! Well, he failed, got sent to motivation platoon and I believe was discharged and sent home. The recruit should never have joined the Marine Corps.

On another occasion we were practicing our drilling. It was a warm day and we had been training hard. All of a sudden, one of our recruits yelled, threw his rifle down and took a swan dive head first into the concrete drill field!. They took him away and we never saw him again. Once again the Marine Corps was not for everyone, but it was meant to separate the weak individuals. I now hear that Drill Instructors are not allowed to discipline trainees. It's so sad that it's come to that.

II was one of four who got promoted to PFC (Private First Class) and I was made a squad leader. SSGT. Saunders was a bit disappointed that I had earn the rank being that I was going into the reserves. He told me that he wish that the promotion had gone to a full time Marine, but he did say I earned it.

A memorable part of my Marine Corps training came when it was time to do water training. This consisted of going to the pool and learning how to use our uniforms as floating equipment. They also found out who couldn't swim and yes you guessed it. I couldn't swim! They took us none swimmers to the side and instructed us on how to float in the water Then we were ordered into the deep part of the pool and told to stay until ordered to get out. I floated and I did the doggie paddle and I was worried, but as luck had it. The company was behind schedule and I was ordered out of the pool immediately. I passed the swimming test! When I arrived at Camp Lejuene, I practice my swimming and got good at it.

My next stop was Camp Lejuene, North Carolina. My MOS (Military Occupational Specialty) was as an 0441 (a logistics clerk). However, as is usually the case with the military, I worked in logistics while being trained at Camp Lejuene. When I finished my training at Camp Lejuene, I was reassigned to the Naval Station in Norfolk, Virginia, and was trained in supply. I was finished, released and sent back home to begin my responsibilities as a reservist. Then when I got to my reserve unit, at Fort Schuylar, in the Bronx, I worked the supply cage.

My return from Camp Lejuene to New York City was a memorable moment. I was given a bus ticket to return to New York, but I was broke and I didn't get any pay when released. I traveled by bus from Camp Lejuene, to New York City, which was almost a nine hour trip. No money, and in uniform. When I got to the bus terminal in New York City, I picked up my duffle bag and started to walk outside.

I was trying to figure out how to get home. All of a sudden a military patrol vehicle showed up and asked what I was doing. I told them that I was going to try and get a free ride on the train. One of the MPS ordered me to go back inside and call someone to come get me. He said that the area had a lot of unsavory characters who took advantage of anyone in uniform. He gave me some change for a phone call and I called my mom. She called my friend Carlos and they came to pick me up. While I waited I had a couple of shitheads try running scams on me. The MP was right and the lord was looking out for me. Mami and Carlos showed up to take me home and I told mami that I was starved. She bought me two slices of pizza and a soda. I was home and safe! A slice of pizza back then was 25 cents! The slice was Hugh, lol. Those were the days my friend.

My reserve time was fun and I met some interesting characters. I laugh because I think some of my fellow Marines were cops and some, where on the other side of the fence. We had some adventures to remember; like when we went to the Bear Mountain area for winter field exercises. It was cold and we usually had to sleep inside our shelter halves. We learned to take our boots off while we slept, so that our feet would stay warm when we put them on again. Another area was cold weather training in Fort Drum, New York. Wow, I will remember that cold forever, as I also remember a couple of Marines who were left at Fort Drum with frost bite. I've never been so cold or maybe what trained me for the cold was apartment 3A, lol.

On January 26, 1977, my first son Albert was born. As is usually the case, I met many good Marines, but I never stayed in touch with any of them after I got hired by the Border Patrol. My favorite Sgt got me a job at Hellenic Lines in Manhattan, especially when I needed it most. I remember one day during an office Christmas party, Sgt was drinking pretty heavy, and when he went to sit down, the chair slid from under him and he fell back. He never spilled a drop of his drink! Lol.

I was again in training in 1977, at Norfolk, Virginia with my Bronx Unit. When we returned from the field some of the guys were singing Elvis songs, so we all jumped in and started singing. The moment we finished, one of the guys who was there singing told us the sad news, that the King was dead. Another one of those moments that you'll remember where you were and what you were doing when the sad event happened.

I was a bills of lading clerk at Hellenic Lines and then was hired by a large bank on Walls Street. My duties were working as an armed security guard. I worked there with my mentor and best friend Ruben who also wanted to get into law enforcement. We thought we were cops, lol. I was then transfer to Citibank/Citicorp Center, where I continued as a security officer. However, I got laid off, then rehired at an accounts billing section for the bank. I would sit for hours and look at checks received and apply the money to that company's account. It was ok for awhile and I made some great friends, but watching that microfiche machine was hard on the eyes. I was able to transfer to the mailroom, which was great because I went to all the departments and met new people. Those of you who know me, know that I love to talk!

I had taken and passed the New York City Police Department test, passed their physical exam, but was later notified that I had to be nineteen years old on the date of the written test and I was only seventeen. I can't think of "what if"? I wouldn't change anything that has happened to me, so I know my life went where the lord wanted it to go.

It was at a Boxing gym on the lower East Side, where I was taught by Papo, Ruben's brother. He was and is an amazing instructor and motivating human being. I was also the quick human heavy bag when someone needed to spar. Yes, I raised my hand many a times, lol. I am surprised that I am not punchy. My friend Papo was voted into the Connecticut Boxing Hall of Fame in 2021. He deserved it!

601 W. Broadway

2323 Cambreleng

Firehouse 176st

P.S 58

Public Library 176ˢᵗ

CHAPTER 4

During this time my best friend, karate instructor/boxing instructor and mentor Ruben Gonzalez had also given me an application for the United States Border Patrol. I had applied for several federal law enforcement tests and finally got a break. I passed the Border Patrol exam and was scheduled for an interview. After six months I was offered a position with the United States Border Patrol. I was to report to El Paso, Texas, but I almost lost this opportunity! It was also during this time period when I started to learn how to box.

I had taken two tests and as I prepared to leave for El Paso, Texas, I received another letter saying that I had not pass the exam. I was angry and didn't know what to do, since I had already given my resignation at work. I got lucky because one of my friends was a Customs Agent and had a friend who was an Immigration Agent. He took me to see the INS agent and I showed the agent the two letters. The INS agent advised me to respond to the letter of acceptance and ignore the other letter. He explained that the left hand and the right were doing the same task, but didn't know enough to talk with each other. My first lesson with the federal system. Plus when you are told no, try and never settle for the word no.

I already had my oldest son Albert Miguel Ortiz, when I accepted the Border Patrol position. My intentions were to go through the academy and then go get my wife and son. Tio Willie drove me to the bus depot where I caught the Trailways bus and bought a ticket to El Paso, Texas. My ex-wife, my son Albert, Tio Willie and mami accompanied me to the bus depot and I said that I would see them soon.

It was very hard for me watching my family get further away as the bus departed the station. A lady on the bus told me that what I was doing for my family was important, and that I would see them again. I've always been lucky to meet very spiritual people during my life. That was my departure from the Bronx and New York City. Mami always taught me that when a door opens, go in right away because it may never open again. So now my adventures with the United States Border Patrol.

Taking the Border Patrol job meant an increase in what I was earning annually in the bank. I got an increase just taking the job. I was lucky or blessed again. I arrived in El Paso, Texas early Monday morning, on November 6, 1978 and took a taxi to the El Paso Sector Headquarters.

We were sworn in and taken to get our motel rooms since we would be staying a week before being sent to the academy. They took us around to the Sears where we could buy green rough duty trousers. We needed to bring money with us because the initial cost for lodging, meals, etc, came out of our pockets. We would get paid while at the academy, but within two weeks after arriving there.

At the motel I shared a room with Louie and Jose. We were on a tight budget and had to make it last until we got our first pay check at the academy. We went as a group to eat at a place on Montana Avenue not far from the motel. After we sat down I noticed that the waiter had brought some type of chip and a dipping type of sauce. I watched a couple of the guys eating it with no problem, so I dipped my chip and holy chip! Some of the guys had a good laugh, but I didn't touch that again for a while. That was my introduction to a food called chile. I do eat hot chile now in my older age, lol.

I listen to oldies, salsa and country western music while growing up in the Bronx. My favorite male vocalist was Marty Robbins and my favorite song was "El Paso". I asked about Rosa's Cantina and was told that the place did exist. So thanks to Louie who had a vehicle, I got to see Rosa's Cantina! I've been there a few times now, but that was a proud moment out in the West town of El Paso. We also got a tour of the border and met some very colorful agents. One of them named, yep you guessed it, Cowboy.

We were flown to Jacksonville, Florida a week after being sworn in. Then we boarded a bus that transported us to Glynco, Georgia, where we entered the Federal Law Enforcement Training Center. I was a member of the 129th session. This academy was the training academy for all federal agencies with the exception of the FBI. A few years later the DEA academy was moved to Virginia. We were lucky because we got to live in the new town homes, where three of us had a room each. Years later they stuffed more people into those town homes.

My roommates again were Louie and Jose since we were going back to the same sector. I think we started with 40 plus trainees, but loss many before the training was over. We were there during a tough time because we were away from our families through Thanksgiving, Christmas and the 1979, New Year's celebration. This was tough on the guys that were married and had families. I was one of them, but I wasn't going to quit. I had already made a commitment that this step was for my family.

It was a very intensive academy and the Border Patrol was very strict, more than all the other agencies. I enjoyed it, and it was a lot easier then Marine boot camp, but academically it was hard.

We had a room, free meals and if we were ahead of the homework on weekends, the town of Brunswick, Jekyll Island and St. Simon's were fun places. We partied, especially during Christmas and New Years Eve. This was the time of disco and I could dance, but the king of dancing and picking up those Georgia Peaches was Juan "The Man" (RIP). A Cuban raised I believe in New Jersey or New York. He was a magnet for the ladies and very smooth. He was also a great guy with all of us, and I got a chance to work with him as a Criminal Investigator, for INS at the Miami, Florida District Office. Unfortunately, I lost my friend to a massive heart attack in 2016. Much too early my dear friend. I did get to speak with Juan on his cell a few days before he passed. We ended our conversation with "we'll talk again when you have time, but that time never happened.

I did real well with the Physical training, self-defense, firearms and the academics. However, I hated the driving course! When we arrived at the driving course, one of the instructors asked for all the New Yorkers to raise their hands. I was one of them. He stated that we were going to be horrible out there since we never owned a vehicle. The joke was on him because I did own a vehicle, I just didn't drive a lot and I didn't like driving. The first thing they did was to take us around the fast course at the rate of speed expected for us to drive.

My luck I got an instructor known as Action Jackson as my driver. Let me say this. He took me around twice and when I got out of the car, my ass stayed puckered to the seat. Then we did the skid pad and holy shit I was horrible at first. Luckily for me it was the last course of the day. I got to the town house and I had to sleep for a while, before I went to the chow hall. I get motion sickness, so driving fast and making my vehicle go in circles did not help.

I did pass the course, but I remember one moment that I want to share. During the fast course the instructors would push you and yell into your vehicle radio. I believe mine was number 10 and all I could hear was faster number 10, hit the apex number ten, etc. One day while driving the course one of the instructors was standing at a curve, yelling for me to hit the apex. I didn't dare get close for fear of hitting him. He continued to yell and I got so frustrated that I pulled over. He came running to my vehicle yelling at me and asking why couldn't I hit the apex. I yelled back at him telling him that I didn't want to freaken run him over! He looked at me, quieted down and walked away. I didn't get bothered much after that.

I was at the academy when my best friend Ruben showed up with the 130th session. I now had a friend at the academy. It served me well being that I was going to need him as a witness at a later time in the academy. Overall my training and time at the academy was a great one.

We did have some shitheads instructors who really bought into the idea that trainees where worthless. It was the old Marine boot camp of treating trainees like shit. However, I was always outspoken and I believed in defending others, plus I knew we had more rights than a Marine Recruit . One day two instructors from another class were giving our instructors a break. They were talking to us, but not being very nice. One of our classmates said something and a bad word escaped his lips. He immediately apologized to our female classmate, but that wasn't good enough for the two instructors.

They asked him to apologize and he did. Then they told him to get up and apologize, which he did. Then they told him to apologize to the class and that was enough for me. I stated to them that he had already apologize and why was it necessary for them to belittle him. One of them came over and told me to mind my business. I stood up and told him that it was my business when he started belittling our classmate. The instructor approached me like he was going to get physical with me and I told him that would be a bad idea.

They wrote me up, but our law instructor heard what happened and had me write it up also. He then called a meeting with the acting Chief. They could've thrown me out, but the chief scolded me, but also scolded the two instructors telling them that they were the instructors and should have shown more professionalism. I won that one, but it wasn't the end.

One day I was walking with my friend Ruben and leaving the cafeteria. I spotted the two shithead instructors, looked at them, but kept my mouth shut and continue talking to my friend. Later that day my law instructor told me that a complaint had been filed against me by the two instructors for having verbally insulted them in the cafeteria. Something that I had not done. However, I had my witness and again had to write memo to the Chief explaining that I did notice the instructors, but that I never spoke with or to them and that I had a witness to that effect. I always dreamed of meeting those two shitheads and really verbally insult them.

Another incident started making me understand that although I held law enforcement officers on a pedestal. They were humans with all the prejudices of any other person. We were at Pam's, which was a Bar/grill off base operated by a guy named Bob, who named the place after his wife Pam. He let us know that he was making a run to FLETC. He had several vehicles and this one was a school bus. So a few of us loaded up and went to the back. Bob waited for other students. Well two white guys get on the bus, and sit on the front seat. One of them turns around and says "wow, wetbacks in the back". A lot of our class members were Hispanics.

One of our guys tells them that these supposed wetbacks were his friends and he should watch how he spoke. The young idiot tells our classmate "Well, too bad you have a bad choice of friends"! My classmate then tells the idiot the shithead that his friends were also veterans of Vietnam. However, stupid wouldn't stop. I sat behind him and told him that he shouldn't pick on my classmate because he was dangerous. He told me to screw myself. So I went back to my seat. We notice that Bob was driving fast to get us to our town houses. Well, as we departed the bus, everyone took a shot at stupid's chest. That was one more example of bigotry by a future law enforcement officer.

I graduated from the academy on March 1979. I went home to visit my spouse, my son and mom and to prepare to leave for my first duty assignment. I had a feeling that my spouse wasn't going to come with me, but she didn't say anything then. I had agreed to helped my classmate Jose drive his belongings to El Paso, Texas. We departed New York City and headed to my next chapter in life. So far this little ole New York Rican was going to make his dream come true.

I helped Jose drive his conversion van which was loaded with his belongings. He left space in the middle for us to take turns sleeping. Luckily we were both short. We had a cooler with sodas and all kinds of munchies. We had gallons of water. The bottle water of today was not available yet. It was my first time behind the wheel, but my second time going the 2,184 miles from New York City, to El Paso, Texas.

As I stated before, I was not a relaxed or confident driver. The miles looked like they would never finish and I had to drive at night because I got sleepy during the day. That was ok with Jose because he rather sleep when it was dark. I remember there was lots of desert. I was a good driver or I should say that I kept the vehicle straight most of the time, but we did have one adventure.

I was driving and I looked down at the gas gauge. It was showing a quarter tank and Jose was sleeping. I remember passing an exit where I believe I saw a gas sign, but I didn't remember how far. However, I panicked because I wasn't sure how far a quarter tank would get you and I didn't know how far the next gas station was. So I did what I got pretty good at doing as an agent. I decided to cross the medium, which was something I got good at doing when I shouldn't.

The problem was that it had rained pretty hard and I never thought that I would sink the tires into the mud. Well, I got stuck and then I woke up Jose. When he realized what I had done, he started yelling at me and asked why didn't I wake him. I told him I didn't think I was going to get the van stuck.

Anyway, now we had to figure out how to get the van out. Then something happened that endeared me to the southwest. A cowboy in a pickup driving the opposite way stops in front of us, goes to the back of his truck and pulls out a chain. He had his girlfriend in the truck and I think I saw a smirk.

He handed me the chain and told me to tie it to the front and that he would pull us out. I wrapped it to the front and the cowboy tied it to the back of his truck. He got in and pulled us out. I took the chain off the front and gave it back to him. Them Jose and I got some money together and offered it to him for his help. He refused it politely.

He told me to help someone down the road if someone needed help. We insisted again on him taking the money and told him "well use it for beer". He showed us the back of his truck and says, I have plenty of beer. He bid us farewell, good luck and drove away. We got to the gas station that I had passed and we still couldn't get over the cowboy's hospitality. I continued to drive after gassing up and had to promise Jose that I wouldn't cross a medium without consulting him first. We arrived in El Paso and I helped Jose drive his van to the apartment he rented and would be living in with his family.

Then he and Louis drove me to my new home. The town of Truth or Consequences, New Mexico! I went from 8 million people to 8,000! The town had changed its name from Hot Springs to Truth or Consequences. Yes, it was named by Ralph Edwards, who created several television shows, including Truth or Consequences, which was hosted by Bob Barker. I kept thinking I was being paid back for something I had done wrong in life, lol. I shared an apartment with my classmate Jeff until I found my own place. I think I lived with Jeff for about two weeks. When I got to TorC, I called my wife to make plans to get them, but she had made a decision that she would not be joining me.

That was a tremendous shock for me and I couldn't stop crying. If not for my mom making me understand that I was also doing the move for my son, I would've return to New York. I am glad I listened to mami and as always she guided me in the right direction. So in March of 1979, I walked into the Truth or Consequences Border Patrol Station, which was a checkpoint on I-25, north of TorC. I was assigned the day shift and I got a welcome that I will never forget.

One of the older agents tells me "Boy, there are three things we hate out here. A Nigger with a badge, a Spic with a gun and a Yankee with a u-haul, and you got two strikes boy". I've always been a fighter and I was taught to respect, but to expect it back. So being that I wasn't going to keep quiet, I told him off.

He was my first journeyman and he wrote me up good, except for me telling him off. That was ok because I wasn't just going to take this from this moron.

He opened his mouth again one day, but not as bad as the first. I did give him a nickname that I used for many years, lol. One day we drove into town and saw an illegal alien hide from us. He stops the vehicle and looks at me and says "well, what the fuck are you waiting for"? I got out and gave chase. I caught the alien and brought him back to our vehicle. When I secured the alien, I looked at the agent and stated "I must be your freaken hunting dog"!

One day I was talking about the good looking women in the town, being that I was headed for divorce. Agent Neanderthal starts to warned me about hitting on the women in town. He stated that the cowboys wouldn't like that. I told him to mind his business and let me worry about the women and the cowboys. The last one was a dozy. One morning I walked in to start a morning shift and he asked me how I was going to vote? I didn't know there was an election and I told him so. He states that Puerto Ricans were going to vote for statehood, stay a common-wealth or go independent. I told him in a not too nice manner, "listen shithead, I am a New York Rican and I don't give a shit how the people of Puerto Rico vote. He never bothered me again with stupid comments.

Another of the senior agents was also pretty shitty with me. Unfortunately, I would be assigned to work midnights with this agent many times. He would walk in, greet everyone, except me and then sit down to read the paper. He wouldn't talk to me except when he would tell me "let's go", and we would get in the vehicle and check the highway for walkers. One night we answered a sensor and made a stop on the vehicle that set off the sensor. He approaches the driver, pulls her out and proceeds to take her to the trunk. I was taking out the aliens, when I saw him walk her to the back with his hands in his pockets, and ordered her to open the trunk.

I put the alien back and put my hand on my weapon. He tells me to get my hand off my gun and I tell him "pay attention to what you are doing". The driver opens the trunk and there are two more aliens in the trunk. I take the aliens out of the trunk and continue with the ones in the vehicle. I am doing everything while he watches.

He drives the patrol car back to the checkpoint and I drive the load vehicle.

After processing the aliens, he threatens me by saying, "when the PAIC comes in, I will tell him about you putting your hand on your gun". I responded with "I survived New York City and I am not going to get killed because you are freaken lazy and open a trunk with your hands in your pocket"!

When the PAIC walked in, the shithead left and never mentioned anything. He always did his overtime with a pencil. So I talked with the PAIC and asked him if I was wrong? The PAIC tells me that in all his years he never had to draw his weapon? When he noticed that I wasn't going to accept that answer, he said that I did nothing wrong. That next night we met again and I asked the agent "how come you didn't talk to the PAIC"? He says just don't? What the ???

When I finally passed my probation status and became a permanent agent, I told the agent that I had made my list of the ten biggest assholes in my life and that he had the first three slots, lol. I called him asshole until I was transferred from TorC. One day I am teaching at the academy and who shows up? Yes, asshole! Well he didn't last long as a detailed instructor because he was horrible with the students.

I had some colorful characters as journeymen, but I also had a few good agents that taught me well and treated me well. The first was Richard. He gave me advise that was always practical, useful and easy to remember. During my career I used his advise and passed it on to younger agents.

Another agent was Phil. One day I was about to put my hands on a dumb agent who almost pushed me out the door. I got thrown out by Phil and instructed to get in the patrol vehicle. He talked with me and made me understand that if I hit the idiot, he would win and I would lose my job and probably get charged for assaulting the idiot. He asked me what my interests were and when I told him. He advised me to go see Tony Tafoya (RIP). Tony ran the boys scouts and the bingo hall in TorC. I went there after my shift and asked Tony if I could teach his scouts martial arts and boxing. He led me to the back room of his hall, opened the door and told me it's yours. When I asked how much, he stated free, just teach the kids.

I fixed the back room, with heavy bags, etc, and started teaching. It was a great way for me to let off some steam. I have thanked Phil many times since I returned to the area.

Things got better as the years passed and I got along well with them all. I started forming Christmas dinners for the agents and our wives and other social events, but those activities stopped after I transferred out.

The best thing that happened to me in Truth or Consequences, was meeting my soul mate Rosemary. Rosemary was married and divorced from a cop with the TorC Police Department. We met one day while I was sitting at the apartment I was renting. There was a fire in the area, and she and a co-worker drove by as I sat outside and petted a dog I was taking care for one of my classmates. I waved to her and she waved back. When I went to work that evening I made a mention of a beautiful gal driving a white Volkswagen Rabbit.

My second line supervisor says "that's Rosemary and she works with my daughter". The great thing about small towns, is that everybody knows everyone, lol. I got her phone number from him and we courted for a few months by phone, before we went on our first date. Her dad was ill and she would go home and help take care of him. I was hooked on this beautiful woman! On our first date, she picked me up at about mid-night because I was working a 4pm-12 mid shift.

At midnight a white vehicle drives up, I look and I say go ahead. I notice she said something, but I couldn't hear her. I walk down the stairs and told her again " go ahead". She said again something and when I got closer, she says "I came to pick you up"! I almost waved my future wife away. She always says that if I would have waved her through one more time, she was going to leave. The guys never let me forget what I did, lol.

Rosemary helped me raise my oldest son Albert, who still calls her mom today and she gave birth to our son Gabriel Jose Ortiz, born June 6, 1982, in Las Cruces, New Mexico. We got married on May 16, 1981 and she has been my heart and soul. My mom was present when we got married and she and Rosemary got along like mom and daughter. They were the two most important women in my life.

I applied to teach at the Federal Law Enforcement Training Center (FLETC). On September 1984, I was assigned to the Physical Techniques Department. I conditioned classes with running, weights and classroom workouts.

My instructions also included defense techniques, baton training, pressure points strikes, etc. I was pretty good and started being used by the FLETC permanent staff to teach other agencies' recruits. The perks of the job was that we received all types of training and got certified with the training. It was a great way to build up my experience and resume. Again, I met some fine agents which included Dan out of Yuma, Arizona. He taught me how to do my paperwork. It was Dan's helped which landed me the next position, at the Miami Border Patrol Station, Miami, Florida, on September 1985.

We trained a lot of agents from September 1984 through September 1985. I met many along the way and learned that my nickname was "The Tasmanian Devil"! I don't know why, lol. After the detail I returned to TorC, but was given a transfer to Ysleta, Texas at my own expense. We moved to Ysleta which is next door to the El Paso Station, where I worked from June 1985 until September 1985. I was selected as Border Patrol Agent for Miami. The move to Miami opened many doors for me professionally, and I met some great people. Plus this was a paid move.

We took our time and got to visit several places on our way to Florida. One of those visits was to the World's Fair in New Orleans, Louisiana. The family even got to stop and visit Graceland, the home of Elvis Presley! When we finally arrived in Miami, we realized that it was a big city and we got a bit scared. We looked for temporary housing and did some exploring of the area, including the beaches.

My wife fell in love with the beaches, but unfortunately our vehicle was broken into and her purse was stolen. Luckily we had taken the bag that had all our money and other important papers with us. Call it instincts or just plain luck. It was our welcome to South Florida.

Temporary quarters was ok, and we met other families whose hubbies had been transferred also. Before you knew it we had found a home in Lake Forest, Broward County. It turned out to be a great neighborhood where we made lifelong friends. It was right above the Dade/Broward county line, with State Road 441 to the west, I-95 to the east. I was only five minutes from the Border Patrol station.

When I reported for duty at the Miami Border Patrol Station, I found that I would be working out of a trailer again! I walked inside and met the PAIC, Steve Norman (RIP). I would say that Steve was the first good supervisor I worked for.

The duty in Miami was a bit different from what I did at the checkpoint in New Mexico. In New Mexico we mostly apprehended entries without inspection (EWIs), but in Miami I realized I had a lot to learn. My defensive comment to everyone was that I was not a rookie, however, I didn't know anything, lol.

Talk about having to learn so many new things. We caught everything from ship stowaways, visa overstays, etc, and arrested Colombians, Jamaicans, Salvadorans, Nicaraguans, seizing money and drugs. It was great work! Another different and great part of the job was that we did a lot of plain clothes work. We still wore a uniform when we were assigned to work the airport, but just about everything else was plain clothes. We worked with lots of other Federal, State and local agencies.

One such case was when I was dispatched to a call from the Davy Police Department. I responded with my partner that night Agent Gil (RIP), where we arrived at the station and were presented a Colombian who they had arrested shooting up the sky with an AK-47. The officers also had an address and wanted to know if we would be willing to knock on the door of the house on the property. we told them that we would knock on the door for them and see what we found, plus the subject in their custody was illegally in the US.

I knocked on the door and when it was opened, I stuck my foot in the door, identified myself and questioned the individual who opened the door as to his status in the country. He stated that he was in the country illegally. I took him back towards a recliner and asked him if we could search the house for other persons illegally in the country. He agreed to let us search and signed a consent form giving us permission to search. The minute I sat him down, I saw the butt of a handgun under some magazines and I yelled gun!. We found twenty kilos of cocaine, automatic weapons in every room and in every vehicle on the property. Plus, $200,000 cash under a mattress. The seizure made the papers and it was a great hit for Border Patrol.

We still arrested Mexican nationals when we worked places like Immokalee, Homestead, and Belle glades, but when we arrested a Mexican national it was great because they were the only group back then not involved in criminal activities. Our job was also to respond to other organizations like the Florida DMV, where we would get calls when someone tried using a passport to obtain a driver's license. The state Department would call if they were suspicious of someone trying to get an American passport by using a birth certificate that was questionable. We would be requested to assist during the service of arrest and search warrants when the people in question were nationals of other countries. Yes, all kinds of illegal aliens! Wow, what a concept!

Then when our PAIC Steve got a promotion to the Yuma Sector, we got a new PAIC. The new PAIC banged heads now and then being that I was a union shop steward. We went from a great leader to one that had no clue.

One of the best assignments I got to work in 1987, was Vice-President Bush's task force called NIMBUS. This was formed by the older Bush before he got elected President. We worked with every law enforcement agency you could name, and also the different branches of the military.

The officer in charge was a member of the Coast Guard. The military side of the house would do intercepts and interpret the different intelligence gathered and then the enforcement side would follow up the leads created by the intelligence. This position included a temporary promotion. The new PAIC wanted me out of the office so he selected me for the position.

The man in charge of the enforcement side of the house was U.S. Customs Supervisory Special Agent George Nimmoor. George went on to become Special Agent in Charge of the internal Affairs Branch for U.S. Customs. Great person to work for. He turned out to be a great mentor, a great instructor and a great friend. He allowed me plenty of room to think and come up with ideas for our side of the house. George and I still talk during the holidays. Thank you George for being a mentor and a friend.

CHAPTER 5

In September 1988, I was promoted to the position of Special Agent/ Criminal Investigator with the U.S. Immigration and Naturalizations Service (INS). It meant more money, a take home vehicle and I could follow an investigation from start to finish. It also allowed me to be a member of different task forces. One of the memorable task forces had me assigned to the Broward County Sheriff's Office non-traditional organize crime unit. This unit investigated and went after organize crime members of other nationalities other then Italians. My new boss was a lady who was the Assistant District Director for Investigations (ADDI). She was an outstanding supervisor. She expected you to work and she expected that from her supervisors.

Our unit was assigned to work Asian Criminal Organizations. This included, Chinese members, Vietnamese, Laotian, etc. My partner was a Broward County Deputy named Steve. The first thing Steve advise me to do was read and learn the customs of Asians. Their customs differed from Americans, Jamaicans, Haitians, etc. Thanks to his advice, my dealings with the groups we were investigating made my involvement with them easier. A simple thing like don't look at the female when talking to the head of the household prevented me from offending and closing the door to any help from different households.

My task force experience also included being a member of the Fort Lauderdale Police Department's street narcotics unit in 1995. We found that having an immigration agent on these task forces opened a lot of doors and gave the task force a lot of flexibility. This also worked well as a member of the Miami FBI's Joint Terrorism Task Force (JTTF).

One of the task forces was rounding up deportable aliens already with active deportation warrants in the Fort Myers, Florida area with the help of the Fort Myers Police Department. Then in September 1995, I was selected as a Special Agent for the Border Patrol Anti-Smuggling Unit, Tucson, Sector/ Fort Huachuca, Arizona office. We packed up and moved to Arizona and the continuation of my career adventures. My time in the Miami Investigations office allowed me to meet and make friends who I keep in contact with.

My office in Fort Huachuca was a two man station with a supervisor in Tucson. My supervisor was Carol (RIP), Supervisory Special Agent. I believe she was also one of the first female supervisors in the Border Patrol. Her idea in picking me was to have me work undercover investigations. The Border Patrol/INS was different in that the case agent also did the undercover work.

This was hard and could be dangerous, but I did it and it was fun! Carol was a small skinny lady, who smoked like a train, but if you wanted a tough backup, she was it. She didn't last long after she retired, but I will always think of her fondly.

As a criminal investigator I would be notified by the different Border Patrol Stations when their agents apprehended illegal aliens who wanted to work as confidential informants. This was great, but you also had to really watch them because some of them just wanted to be able to do their own smuggling operations with our blessings or avoid jail time. I was pretty good at this and started an undercover case in Douglas, Arizona right away named "Operation Vacancy".

The target was a motel being rented by its owner to a smuggler. The owner figured that if he did it that way, he couldn't be charged for running the motel as a staging area for smugglers. I was introduced by an informant and able to infiltrate a couple of groups working out of the motel. I conducted the investigation for about six months, infiltrated the organization and provided evidence that the paper owner and the legal owner were in partnership of the smuggling operations out of the motel.

The case ended up with convictions of the owner, the guy renting the motel, seizure of several vehicles and the motel. In 1997, I was awarded a special recognition award for "Operation Vacancy".

Smuggling investigations were long and if you also did the undercover work during the case, you had to be very careful that you didn't make a mistake and get caught by the bad guys. I did several cases and in 1998, was assigned to the FBI corruption task force for about a year and a half. The only thing I will write about this time, is that I never believed that we had so many dirty agents, who had compromised their badges, and were at different levels of supervision.

However, when I left the task force I would definitely watch my butt. After the task force, I returned to my anti-smuggling duties. My career with the INS/Border Patrol was fun and I wouldn't trade the experience for anything else.

While living in South Florida, I became a big fan and follower of vocal groups. My friend Chris and I would attend Doo Wop shows promoted at different venues. Some of these groups had original members of famous singing groups from the New York area. We got the bug when we used to watch and listen to a group called

"The Five Boros". These guys were great and I ended buying one of their albums and we were hooked. We would go see their shows and during some of these shows we met and became friends of one group called "Legacy".

I got lucky when one day I was given a call from a cop with the Miami Beach Police Department because I was the duty agent. The officer had information reference some pickpockets working in his area. After taking the information, I recognized his New York accent and I asked him where he was from. He replied that he was from the Bronx, which is where I am from! We started talking about my favorite music, then I started talking about the group shows and about Legacy. When I didn't hear him talk much I asked if he liked doo wop? He answered that he did and then surprised me by telling me that he was the fat white guy who sang with Legacy!

To make this story short he invited me to their next practice. I took my friend Chris with me and we became immediate fans of Legacy. These guys were amazing and they treated us as if we were part of the family. We would attend all their shows and got to meet some pretty big singers when we would get together with them after shows. After relocating to Tucson, Arizona in 1995, I started missing the music I got to love and got this idea that I could start a vocal singing group.

I talked it over with members of Legacy. They gave me ideas, encouragement and their bass singer gave me the name for the group. So welcome "Desert Doo Wop". I placed ads in a Tucson community paper named "The Tucson Weekly" and held auditions. The original members were Robert, originally from Staten Island, Bruce, originally from Brooklyn, Frank originally from Tucson and me. We did our first performance in 1998, about a year after getting together. I must say that we did great! A picture of that first group's personnel can be seen in youtube under "Desert Doo Wop". Frank made the pictures and videos available on youtube. Thanks Frank.

The group had the changing of personnel now and then, but we were active for almost 18 years. The final members were Robert "Bobbyg", his wife Marie, originally from Brooklyn, Lou, originally from Rochester, New York, Robert, originally from Binghamton, New York and me. There were other members, but the last ones mentioned were the last members. It was also the group that got to do more shows at locations where you could rent the theater, tickets were sold by the organization owning the theater, and we would get a cut. We actually had a following. When you get a chance look up Desert Doo Wop on YouTube and you can see some of our performances.

We disbanded in 2013, when I relocated to New Mexico. However, the memories of that part of my musical adventures will last in my mind forever. I had further adventures with my music and continued singing with other groups, but for me there will never be another Desert Doo Wop. I wrote a song named "Window Of Time", which was released with my friend Stevie on lead, Bobby (RIP) sang and created the music, and Bobby's wife Gale. I also sang on the recording and was told by Stevie that it had been a big hit on the Sirius XM50s Bobby DoWop Shop.

Now back to the job. In 2003, things would get crazy for me and our agency. The attack on September 11, 2001, would force the creation of a new agency called "Department of Homeland Security. On November, 2003, we became Immigration and Customs Enforcement (ICE) and Border Patrol became Customs and Border Protection (CBP). The idea was good, but the implementation was a nightmare! We went from knowing our job to not knowing what the agency wanted from us. The word legacy was constantly used, and if you were INS, you didn't care for doing Custom enforcement duties and if you were Customs you didn't want to enforce Immigration laws. The agents received cross training so that we could do each other's job, but it wasn't a very well thought-out Idea.

Another thing was the fighting for what we called grade. The Custom's agency always had better pay grades, but INS was the opposite. So the people who were excited about getting a better pay grade we fighting tooth and nail for every little promotion that was going to be offered in the newly formed ICE. It became more about the grade then doing the job. That got me into trouble with both legacy Custom's personnel and legacy INS personnel.

This time period would test my mental strength and my faith. I had turned over an informant to ICE agents in Nogales, Arizona. The informant got caught doing something wrong and right away stated that I had given him permission to do what he was alleged to be doing. The next thing I know I get a visit from our office of Professional Responsibility (OPR). This was our version of internal affairs. I met with them and contrary to what I used to advise as a shop steward, I did so without a representative present. I didn't think I had done anything wrong, but I knew that when you deal with these individuals, anything you say can be turn around and used against you. So I met them and they questioned me. I told the truth and when they were finished, I left and when home.

Soon after that interview, I was served with a notice that the agency would be seeking to indict me! I was mortified and that night I had the most dangerous time sleeping. Those that know me, know that my integrity and character have always been of the outmost importance to me. Now I was looking at the possibility that I could get fired, prosecuted, incarcerated and lose my pension. It was like I was going to lose everything.

That night I thought of the worst thing anyone can think about. I kept thinking about how I was going to kill myself so my family could at least get my life insurance. I slept in one of the other bedrooms and kept thinking of how to use my service weapon. However, several things kept coming into my mind which saved me and my family from such a cowardly act. First, I knew it was against God's law to kill myself. Second, I knew I had done nothing wrong. I had documented every action taken during all my cases. Later I learned that the informant in questioned had been given an extension on their work permit and was now working for the agents who accused me of wrong doing. I found that his information had been used to get a court order for a wire-intercept, which meant that they lied to the judge who signed the court order.

The next day after that dreadful night, I met with my supervisor and turned over my service weapon. I was already assigned desk duties, so I didn't need a weapon since I would not be making any arrests.

I reached out to several good friends who I knew could guide me. The first thing I was asked by my friend George was "who did you piss off"? I knew the answer to that. So I hired an attorney and made sure that I did all the leg work to make sure he had plenty of evidence to prove that I was not guilty of what the government was alleging. When we met with the US Attorney, she states that they knew I had not gained any money from any illegal acts. She then stated that the government was not gaining anything also, but my attorney told her that we would show how wrong the government was in trying to prosecute an innocent agent.

They served me with a notice that stated, that though they would not go after any prosecution, but they would reserve the right to go after me anytime. I won, but I knew that I would not be happy working with such idiots. So I worked for a while and when I knew I was ready to retire, I did. I've always knew that when you worked for Uncle Sam, you worked for an ungrateful master. So on September 30, 2005, I retired and have not looked back. I've met some good people along the way, but those that tried to screw me know enough to stay away from me.

I knew what I wanted to do after retirement, so I put together a self-defense training program for women. The program was named Individual Defensive and Protective Instincts. A few years later I restructured it, I took out the private investigative service and made it a non-profit. I had many students and continued to teach at the Dona Ana Community College, Community Education section, until the classes were stopped due to budget constraints. I finally had to realize that I was getting too old to continue getting hit by students. So at the age of 64, I stopped teaching. I would start teaching again in 2022, at the age of 67! It's hard to get that experience out of my blood. So I do it cautiously, lol.

I retired about five years before my wife. So after two years of not working, I was told that the U.S. Marshall's Service was looking for part-time detention officers. I went, interviewed and was hired. This was another exciting time in my life.

I worked with and met some great Deputy Marshalls, plus some great retired former Arizona State Police Officers. The duties were receiving inmates from the Federal prisons who had court hearings. We would move them to the different floors using the detention elevators. The Deputy Marshall assigned to that courtroom, would meet us and take possession of the inmate. Once they had they hearing, the Deputy Marshall would call the cell block and we would pick up the inmate. We worked in teams of two. The inmates were always secured with leg and hand shackles, but we never took a chance that they may try to escape.

A few months after I started working the cell block, the Border Patrol start bringing in 70 illegal aliens a day for an initial in front of a judge. They would plea and a record would be created for each one. The next time they were caught the individual would be prosecuted. I started noticing that out of 70 aliens a day, about 10 of those were a bit on the hardcore side. These were individuals who were brought to the US as children, but whose status in the US was never adjusted. Lots of tattoos, and attitude. The other detention officers were curious as to how I could handle the smell of these individuals who had not had a chance to shower and change clothes. I told them it was like I was back in the Patrol, lol.

I did this work for about two years and then I got lucky and got hired as a Court Security Office (CSO). This had me in the courthouse, but walking the floors, patrolling outside and working certain gates. I worked the midnight shift being that I was a new hire. I didn't mind and I did this work until Rosemary retired and we prepared to move to New Mexico. The move to New Mexico also threw us another responsibility. We bought the house where my wife was born and raised at in New Mexico. We had it remodeled and where going to use it as a place to stay after we came back home from travelling. Well our lord had other plans for us. We took custody of my youngest son's daughter and her new born brother! So we were raising kids again. We would get comments from family members that we were heroes for taking these children. My response has always been what would happen if I show up at the pearly gates and I have to explain why I didn't try taking care of these two children that were my blood and needed our care.

These children would have gone into foster care and probably separated. My wife and I have taken measures so that they have something should we die. Plus we did it to protect them from anyone who thinks they can come here and displace these kids. That's not going to happen.

The home was remodeled, but we wanted to keep the blood heritage of the house. So we didn't tear it down. The farm was owned by the youngest of my wife's siblings. The minute we moved in, we knew that the lord had sent us to that house. We moved in with two grand children, had my mom living with us for a while and when she left, my brother-in-law stayed with us for little over a year. So like I mentioned, our home was a safe refuge for a few people. At first it was hard going from Tucson where we were really active, to a small town in New Mexico, where things can be real slow. Luckily I involved myself with different things which kept me busy.

CHAPTER 6

My retirement was anything but boring! I've been busier as a retired individual then when I was employed. My wife and I raising two grand children at our age keeps us busy and I also hear from everyone, that it keeps me young? Oh yea, young, on skates and possibly a heart attack along the way, lol. I pray the lord gives us enough life so my wife and I can see our grandson do things for himself. Though we may not see grand kids from him or our granddaughter because of our age. I still want to see them doing good things and being good individuals.

Because my granddaughter was a student at Hatch Valley High School, I joined the Booster Club. It was fun helping them raise money for different groups, but it was a very high stress activity. It was another gentleman and I as the only males doing the lifting, etc. Then when he no longer had any kids involved at the school, he quit! I stayed, but one day I got really tired and I finally quit. I was much older and I didn't have any kids who at that moment needed me to be involved. I kept asking where are the other males, but we never had any give of their time.

Then I joined the Hatch Chamber of Commerce, where I volunteered to run the vendor's area during Hatch Chile Festival. I gave that adventure my all, lol, but it was just the long ranger again. I did this for two years, but finally quite when I realized that no one was going to help me. It was a tough job for one person. I am finally realizing that as much as I love to help out, I am getting too old to do it alone anymore.

I also wanted to continue studying and possibly getting a college degree. I did attend John Jay College of Criminal Justice in New York, but had to resign in 1973, due to a low GPA. My work and a lack of discipline on my part stopped me from going back after the year suspension. However, I kept taking college courses in the different places where I was working.

After many years. on May of 2019, I earned my Associate Of General Studies, from New Mexico State University! It took almost forty years to get my college Associates Degree, but I did it. My wife asked me if I was going to walk for my graduation? I said hell yea!, lol. It was another example of my never giving up, no matter how long it took me. I have my diploma hanging on my "I love myself wall". That's where I hang many award plaques and yes, my diploma.

So when I speak to kids that may feel disenfranchised. I use my story to show that quitting should never be in their vocabulary. I also like speaking with kids in this community because many are migrant worker's children. So I try to motivate them so they can understand that they can do better than their parents.

I continued working through the years. It was my way of keeping busy besides raising grandkids. I worked for a while with the New Mexico State University as a security officer for their Police Department. This had me work all the football and Basketball games. I did this until the Pandemic hit and then I just resigned. I could still work, but it would be inside the student's dorms. I think that was more dangerous, lol. I loved the job because I was always talking to the folks getting on the line to enter the Arena.

Now I am trying to reinvent myself at my age. I refuse to sit and let the years go by without being active. I believe that if a person doesn't keep motivated, they will get hit by illnesses that will make the final life's chapter a slow painful existence. So my first action was to get training and certified by the John Maxwell Speaking organization. I have all kinds of certifications and I keep them handy so I can show when I am speaking.

I can give my soul mate some of the credit for this not new, but enjoyable career. She has told me numerous times that I love talking so much, I should be a tour guide, lol. so speaking career here I come. I've also done it after retirement. So now I'll do it again, but this time hopefully get paid.

I am starting "Individual Instincts", a speaking company where my target audiences will be youngsters who need guidance in the right direction; abused women and elders. I want to show others that though I was raised by a single mom, with limited finances. I did dream and followed those dreams. You and only you are responsible for achieving the things in life that you need to achieve. No one owes us anything. Like I used to tell teens; though society already has you counted out, only you can strike out if you listen to them and allow yourself to fail. My motto again is that being a victim is not an option.

I consider myself really blessed with lifelong friends. The first one is my special friends, karate instructor/boxing instructor is Ruben. I've mentioned Ruben in the book when we worked for Citibank and then followed each other to the Border Patrol. We ended up working in Miami, Florida. Now I live in New Mexico and he is in Texas. In July, 2020, he called me and told me that he had sent me a package. He said for me to let him know when I got it. The package arrived, I opened it and I was speechless, which for me is saying a lot, lol.

Ruben presented me with a karate Gi, a black belt with the markings of a 4th degree in the Goju Ryu Karate Do discipline, and a picture signed and presented to him by the legendary Karate Master Charles Bonet, Okinawa Karate. Ruben signed this over to me with his title Ruben Goju Ryu Karate Do. Ruben was also my instructor when I earned my black belt in Tae Kwon Do. I learned to box from Ruben's brother Jose "Papo", who recently was inducted into the Connecticut Boxing Hall of Fame! I was always lucky to be surrounded by good amazing role models.

Thanks to facebook, I keep in touch with Ruben and some other special friends. So once again this book is to motivate those that may have been born from the same type environment that many people come from, but work hard and fight to make sure they live the life the lord meant for us.

I think this is the shortest book written, about a guy who has had a rich and wonderful career. I've done many undercover cases, met some interesting individuals. I've had some good cases and I've had a lot of funs during search warrants and arrest warrants. However, I also had a lot of fun besides the job. My adventures into music, with forming a singing group and writing songs, to include one played on the Sirius XM50s, Bobby B. Doowopp shop. God has been good to me. Mami I miss you every day, though I think of you every day and speak with you every day. I will always love you!

Printed in the United States
by Baker & Taylor Publisher Services